THE COMPLETE CLARINET PLAYER

BOOK I

by Paul Harvey.

'By the end of this book, you will be
reading music and playing thirty-four popular songs
including *This Ole House, Rivers of Babylon,
Ob-La-Di Ob-La-Da* and
I'd Like To Teach The World To Sing.'

Paul Harvey

Wise Publications
London/New York/Paris/Sydney/Copenhagen/Madrid

Acknowledgement

I am grateful for the many helpful suggestions given to me about this tutor by *Kathleen Jones*, Principal Clarinet of the Orquesta Sinfonica de Puerto Rico, and Professor of Clarinet at the Conservatorio de Musica, San Juan, Puerto Rico.

Thanks also to Ruth Haines who posed for the photographs.

Paul Harvey.

Exclusive Distributors:

Music Sales Limited
14/15 Berners Street, London W1T 3LJ, England.

Music Sales Pty. Limited
20 Resolution Drive, Caringbah, NSW 2229, Australia.

This book © Copyright 1986, 1994 by Wise Publications
Order No. AM62613
ISBN 0-7119-0877-X

Art direction by Mike Bell.
Designed by Sands Straker Studios Limited.
Diagrams by Mark Straker.
Photography by Peter Wood.
Arranged by Paul Harvey.
Clarinet supplied by Bill Lewington Limited.

Your Guarantee of Quality
As publishers, we strive to produce every book to the
highest commercial standards.
Throughout, the printing and binding of this book have been planned
to ensure a sturdy, attractive publication which should give years of enjoyment.
If your copy fails to meet our high standards, please inform us and we
will gladly replace it.

CONTENTS

About This Book

There is no reason why developing a sound basic technique on an instrument should not be fun. In the past, tutors were predominantly filled with technical exercises, scales and arpeggios, and these are, of course, still available if required. The Complete Clarinet Player, however, covers the same ground, and achieves the same end, using popular songs as the practice material.

Everyone who takes up an instrument is eager to start trying to play songs as soon as possible. This can be a waste of time, or even detrimental, if the songs chosen are not in the right range or key for the stage which the student has reached.

The format of this book ensures that each song which appears has a definite technical purpose.

As each new note is introduced, a minimal technical exercise demonstrates the new finger movement necessary to obtain it. The songs which follow are specially selected and transposed into a suitable key so as to incorporate the new note and finger movement.

Scales and arpeggios are not neglected, but appear within the songs, making the student aware of the reason for practising them. Handel's 'Joy To The World' demonstrates the scale and is used in each key in conjunction with The Beatles' 'Ob-La-Di, Ob-La-Da' to demonstrate the arpeggio.

An important feature of the course which many teachers will welcome is the repetition, a twelfth higher, of songs already learnt in the bottom register, so that the student can relate bottom and upper register fingerings.

No other tutor has anything like enough material devoted to this vital aspect of clarinet technique.

About the Clarinet

The clarinet was invented in about 1700 by J.C. Denner of Nuremberg, Germany. It is a wonderful woodwind instrument, with a single reed and a cylindrical bore, meaning that the tube is more or less the same width throughout except for the bell.

It is most likely that your clarinet is a Boehm System in B♭. Early clarinets had very few keys, but more were gradually added until about 1840, when Klose invented his model based on Boehm's flute system. This is now the standard system everywhere except in Germany.

There used to be clarinets made in lots of different keys, because it was difficult to play sharps and flats on the early instruments. The B♭ clarinet gradually became the most popular, until today when we say "clarinet" we generally mean a clarinet in B♭.

So your clarinet is a transposing instrument, sounding a whole tone lower than concert pitch; that is to say, when you play written C, it sounds B♭ on the piano.

The other important way in which the clarinet differs from other woodwind instruments is that it "overblows a 12th." This means that you play the notes in the bottom register, then open the register key with your left thumb, and the same fingerings will be twelve notes higher. This is because the clarinet has a cylindrical bore; conical instruments like the oboe and saxophone overblow an octave.

To get some idea of what the clarinet is capable of, try to listen to some of the pieces in this "Top Ten" list I've compiled; there are many recordings of them available.

The Clarinet's Top Ten

Mozart:	Concerto
	Quintet (with string quartet)
Weber:	Concertino
	Concerto No. 1
	Concerto No. 2
Brahms:	Sonata No. 1
	Sonata No. 2
	Quintet (with string quartet)
Aaron Copland:	Concerto
Carl Nielsen:	Concerto

In the jazz field you should listen to the work of: *Benny Goodman   Artie Shaw   Buddy de Franco*

There are many other fine players, of course, but those three are the most important to start with.

THE RUDIMENTS OF MUSIC

The notes on the lines:

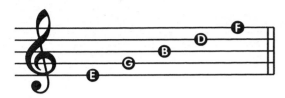

The notes in the spaces:

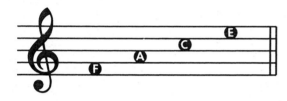

As the clarinet has a big range, it uses lots of *Ledger Lines* below the stave:

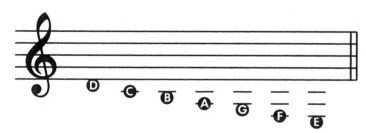

and above the stave:

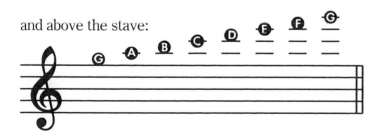

Note Values

A *Semibreve* (or whole note) 𝅝 = 4 counts

A *Minim* (or half note) 𝅗𝅥 = 2 counts

A *Crotchet* 𝅘𝅥 = 1 count

Two *Quavers* (or eighth notes) 𝅘𝅥𝅮𝅘𝅥𝅮 = 1 count

Four *Semiquavers* (or sixteenth notes) = 1 count

Three *Quaver* Triplets = 1 count

A dot after a note lengthens its value by half as much again, so a dotted minim 𝅗𝅥. = 3 counts.

A tie between two notes of the same pitch adds their value together, so 𝅘𝅥 𝅘𝅥 = 𝅗𝅥

Music is divided into sections called *Bars* or measures. The *Time Signature* tells you how many beats there are to each bar:

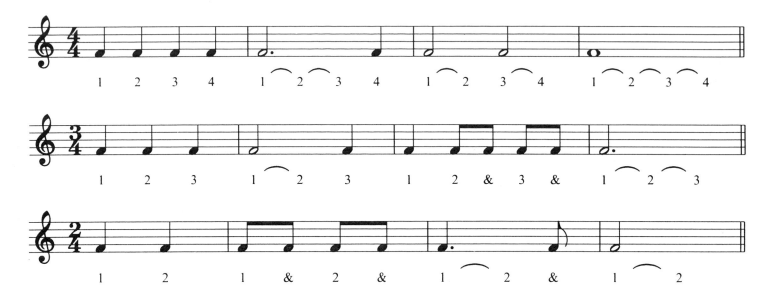

4/4, 3/4 and 2/4 are called simple time, and tell you how many crotchets to a bar.

6/8 is called compound time, and tells you how many quavers to a bar, but it is usually counted two beats in a bar, with three quavers to each beat:

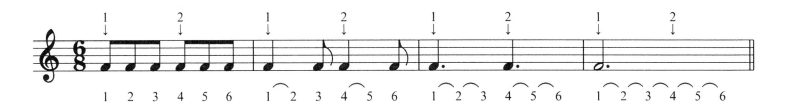

A *Sharp* sign ♯ before a note *Raises* it a semitone or half step.

A *Flat* sign ♭ before a note *Lowers* it a semitone or half step.

A *Natural* sign ♮ before a note cancels out a previous sharp or flat.

These are *Repeat* signs.

Key Signatures will be explained as we go through the book.

Here is an example of the use of repeat signs, and also
first and second time bars:

REPEAT WALTZ
Music by Paul Harvey

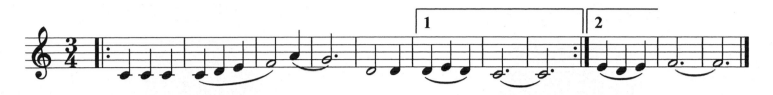

It would be played like this:

D.S. stands for 'Dal Segno', or back to the sign 𝄋
D.C. stands for 'Da Capo', or back to the beginning.

If a song starts with an incomplete bar, the rest of the
bar is made up by the last note, i.e.:

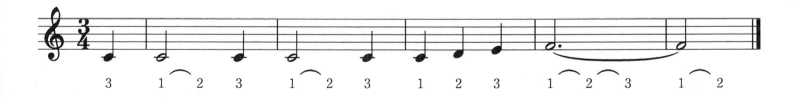

RESTS

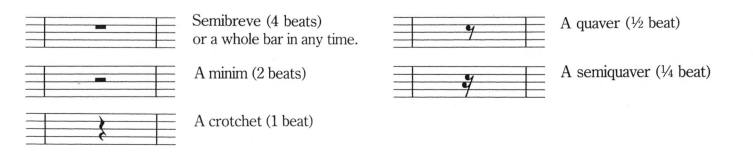

Semibreve (4 beats)
or a whole bar in any time.

A minim (2 beats)

A crotchet (1 beat)

A quaver (½ beat)

A semiquaver (¼ beat)

THE MAJOR SCALE AND CHORD

All songs are based on scales and chords; the most common of these are called major, and are all spaced like this:

The major chord is made up of notes 1, 3, 5 and 8 from the scale:

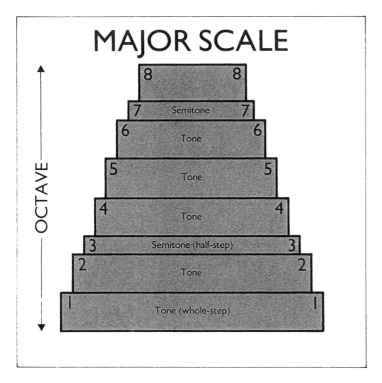

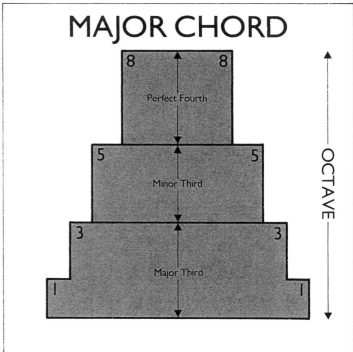

You will learn the scale and chord of two keys in Book 1;

G major

and F major

THE BOEHM SYSTEM CLARINET

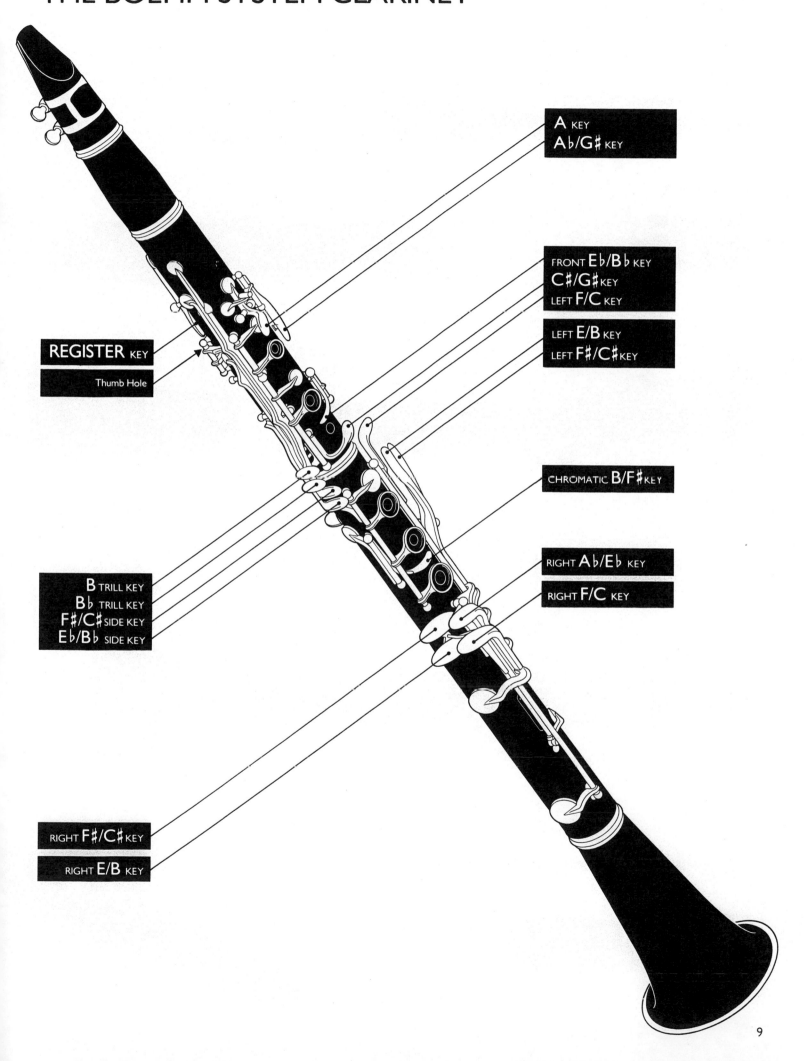

A KEY
Ab/G# KEY

FRONT Eb/Bb KEY
C#/G# KEY
LEFT F/C KEY

LEFT E/B KEY
LEFT F#/C# KEY

REGISTER KEY

Thumb Hole

CHROMATIC B/F# KEY

RIGHT Ab/Eb KEY

RIGHT F/C KEY

B TRILL KEY
Bb TRILL KEY
F#/C# SIDE KEY
Eb/Bb SIDE KEY

RIGHT F#/C# KEY

RIGHT E/B KEY

Session 1: LET'S GET IT TOGETHER

Your clarinet consists of eight parts.

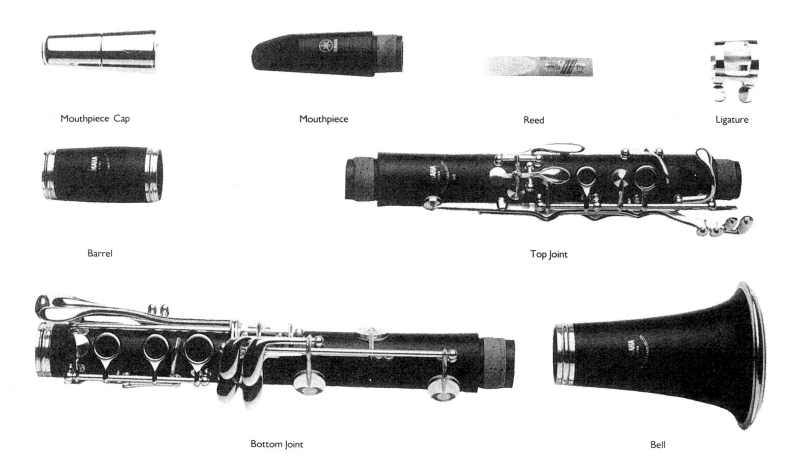

Mouthpiece Cap   Mouthpiece   Reed   Ligature

Barrel   Top Joint

Bottom Joint   Bell

Put cork grease on all the cork joints.
Put the bell on the bottom joint.

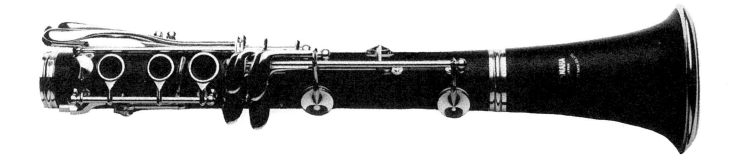

Put the mouthpiece into the narrower end of the barrel.

Put the wider end of the barrel on to the top joint.

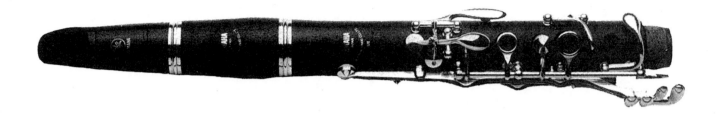

Put the reed on the mouthpeice so that a thin line of black shows over the top.

Put the ligature carefully over the reed.

Do up the screws firmly but not too tightly.

Always put the mouthpiece cap on when not playing, to protect the reed and mouthpiece.

Hold the top joint with your left hand upwards, fingers holding down the rings.

Hold the bottom joint with your right hand downwards.

Put the two joints together, so that the linkage mechanism is lined up.

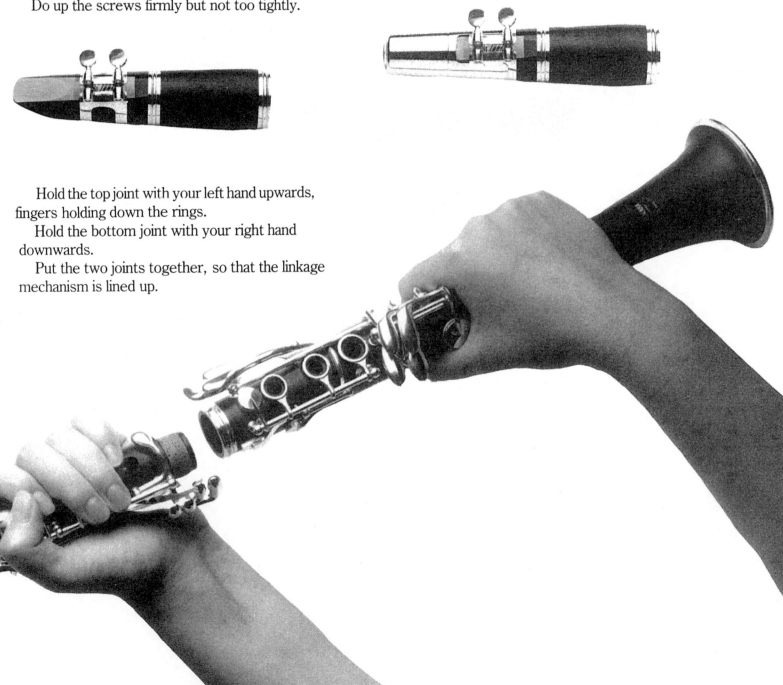

BLOWING YOUR FIRST NOTE

When you see a clarinet standing in a music shop window with nobody touching any holes or keys, it is playing '*Open G*'.

G
1 2 3 4

This is a semibreve or whole note.
It is worth four counts.

Hold your clarinet like this *Just To Practise Blowing This Note*, but remember, this is *Not* the correct hand position for playing anything else.

Place your top teeth lightly on top of the mouthpiece.
Let the reed push your bottom lip over your bottom teeth as you slide the mouthpiece into your mouth.
Close your top lip firmly around the mouthpiece and blow.
Do Not Let Your Cheeks Blow Out.

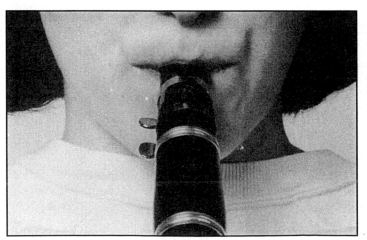

Once you can produce this note, practise starting it with your tongue on the reed, just like singing '*Tee, Tee*'.

This is very important, because your tongue is like a violinist's bow or a drummer's sticks; it makes all your rhythm on the clarinet.

Tee   Tee
1   2   3   4

These are Minims or Half Notes.
They are worth two beats each.

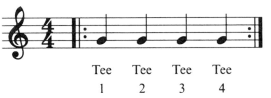

Tee   Tee   Tee   Tee
1   2   3   4

These are Crotchets or Quarter Notes.
They are worth one count each.

Play this one note song which clarinets in shop windows sing:

Please   buy   me, please   buy   me
4   1   2   3   4   1   2   3

When you take a breath *Do Not Breathe In Through Your Nose.*
Keep your top lip on the mouthpiece.
Breathe in by dropping your bottom jaw and taking the air in at the sides of your mouth and under the reed.

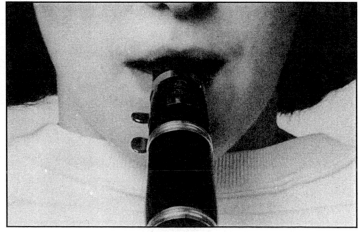

Session 2: GOOD NEWS FOR THE LEFT HANDED

Yes, your left hand is the more important, because it controls the top half of the clarinet.

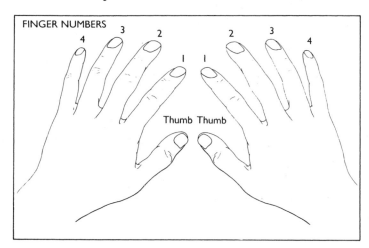

The note above open G is A:

Played by opening this key with finger No. 1 of your left hand.

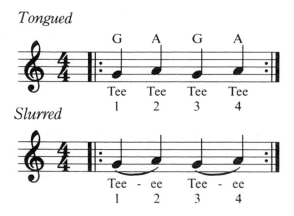

Every time we move to a new note we will practise it two ways: first *Tongued*, then *Slurred*.

Slurred means fingering the new note without tonguing.

Tongued

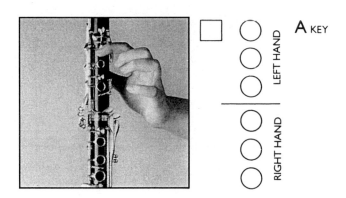

The note below open G is F:

Played by covering the hole on the back of the top joint with your left thumb.

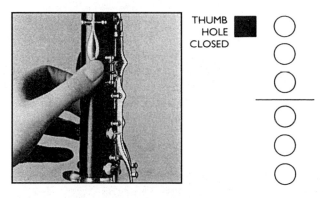

Be careful not to touch the key just above it.

Tongued

Slurred

13

THREE NOTE SONG

By Paul Harvey

There are not many songs on only three notes, so I've written one especially for you.

Session 3: MORE LEFT HAND NOTES

For all notes below F keep your left thumb on the hole at the back.

For E, add finger no. 1 on the first hole.

For C, add finger no. 3 on the hole without a ring. All the top joint is now closed.

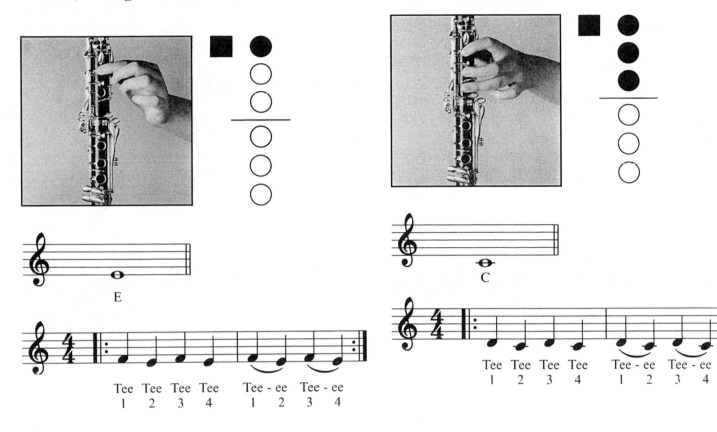

E

Tee Tee Tee Tee   Tee - ee   Tee - ee
1   2   3   4   1   2   3   4

C

Tee Tee Tee Tee   Tee - ee   Tee - ee
1   2   3   4   1   2   3   4

For D, add finger no. 2 on the next hole. Note the wide gap between fingers 1 and 2.

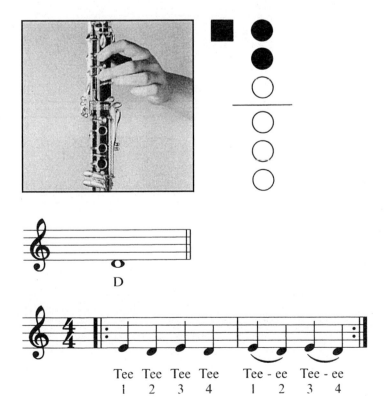

D

Tee Tee Tee Tee   Tee - ee   Tee - ee
1   2   3   4   1   2   3   4

AU CLAIR DE LA LUNE

Traditional

THE BANKS OF THE OHIO

Traditional

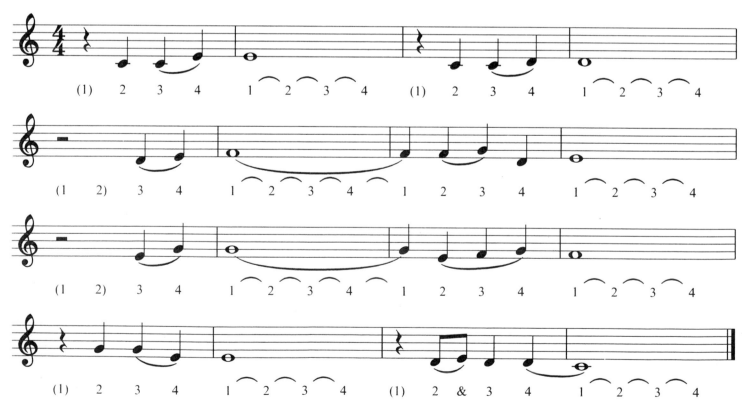

MICHAEL, ROW THE BOAT ASHORE
Traditional

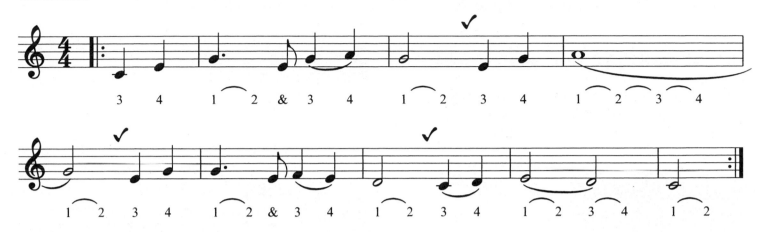

WHEN THE SAINTS GO MARCHING IN
Traditional

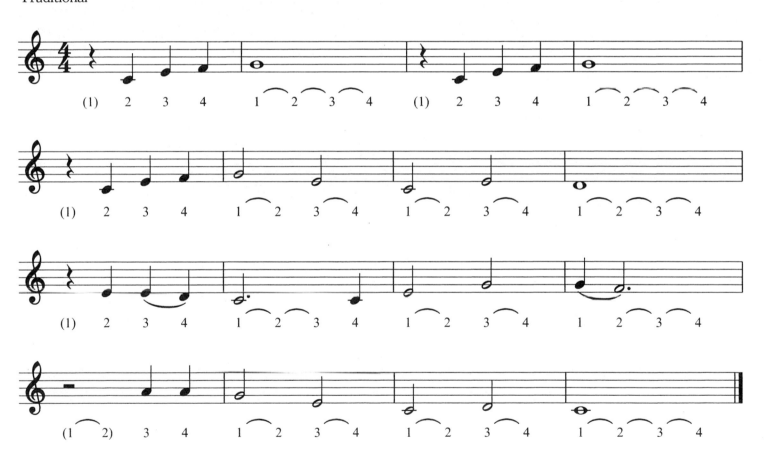

Session 4:
LEFT HAND SONGS WITH ONE MORE NOTE

The flat sign (♭) before a note lowers it a semitone or half step.

The highest note in the bottom register is B♭.

This B♭ is played like A, plus your left thumb opening the register key at the back of the clarinet.

Note that the flat sign applies up to the end of the bar.

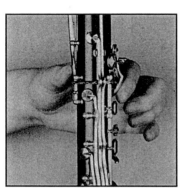

LOVE ME TENDER
Words & Music by Elvis Presley & Vera Matson

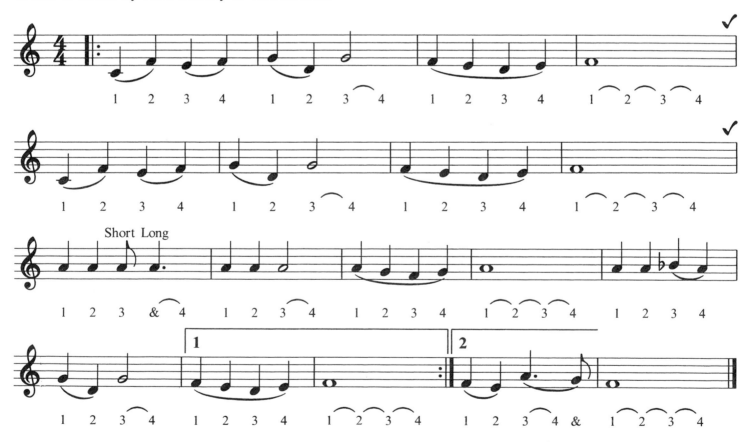

YANKEE DOODLE
Traditional

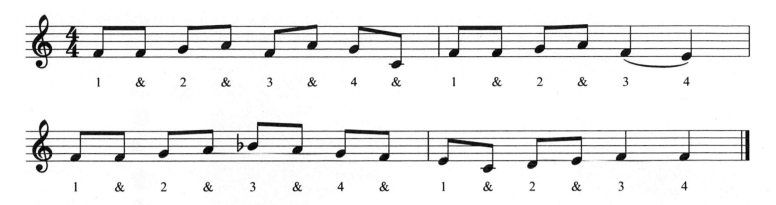

Note the difference between these even quavers (half notes) i.e. "Fish *and* Chips", and the jerky quavers in "Yellow Submarine", i.e. "Sausages 'n' Chips".

YELLOW SUBMARINE
Words & Music by John Lennon & Paul McCartney

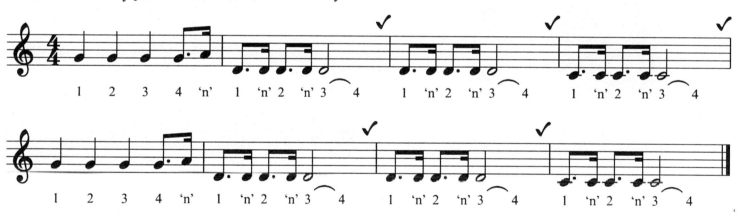

You will be able to play the rest of this song after the next session.

Session 5: YOUR FIRST RIGHT HAND NOTES

For all notes on the bottom joint, all the holes in the top joint must remain covered by your left hand fingers.

First put your right thumb in its supporting position, with the thumb rest over the base of your thumbnail.

To play B, miss out the first hole on the bottom joint, and cover the middle hole with finger no. 2. (Middle finger on middle hole).

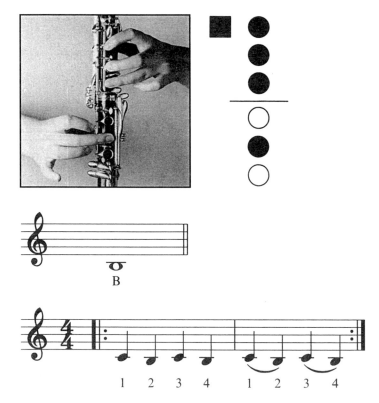

To play A, put finger no. 1 on the first hole, keeping finger no. 2 on the middle hole as well.

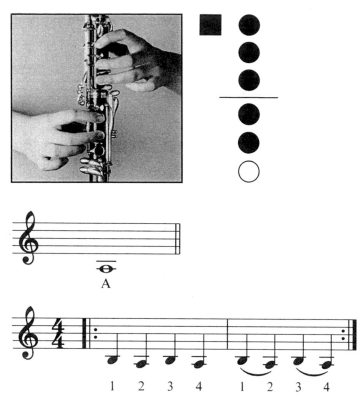

This is low A, an *Octave* (eight notes) below the A you learnt in session 2.

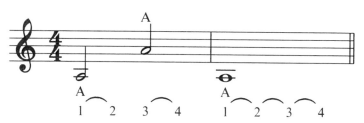

20

GOD SAVE THE QUEEN *(in the key of C major)*
Traditional

THE GRAND OLD DUKE OF YORK
Traditional

YELLOW SUBMARINE *(Complete Version)*
Words & Music by John Lennon & Paul McCartney

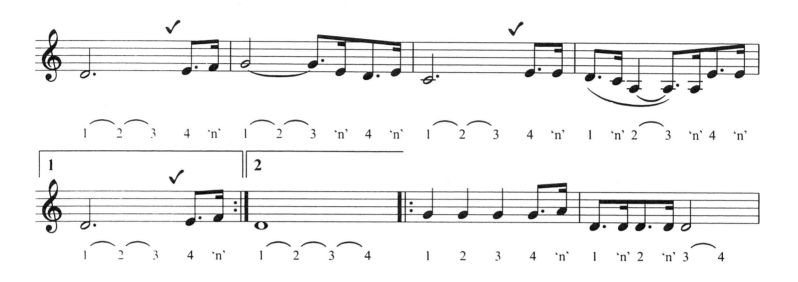

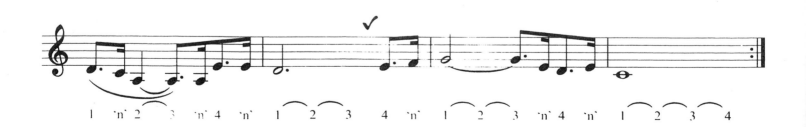

MONEY, MONEY, MONEY

Words & Music by Benny Andersson & Bjorn Ulvaeus

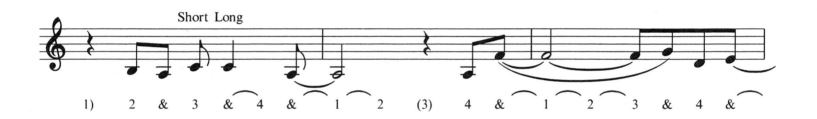

STRANGERS IN THE NIGHT

Music by Bert Kaempfert   Words by Charles Singleton & Eddie Snyder

THE COMPLETE CLARINET PLAYER
PULL OUT CHART

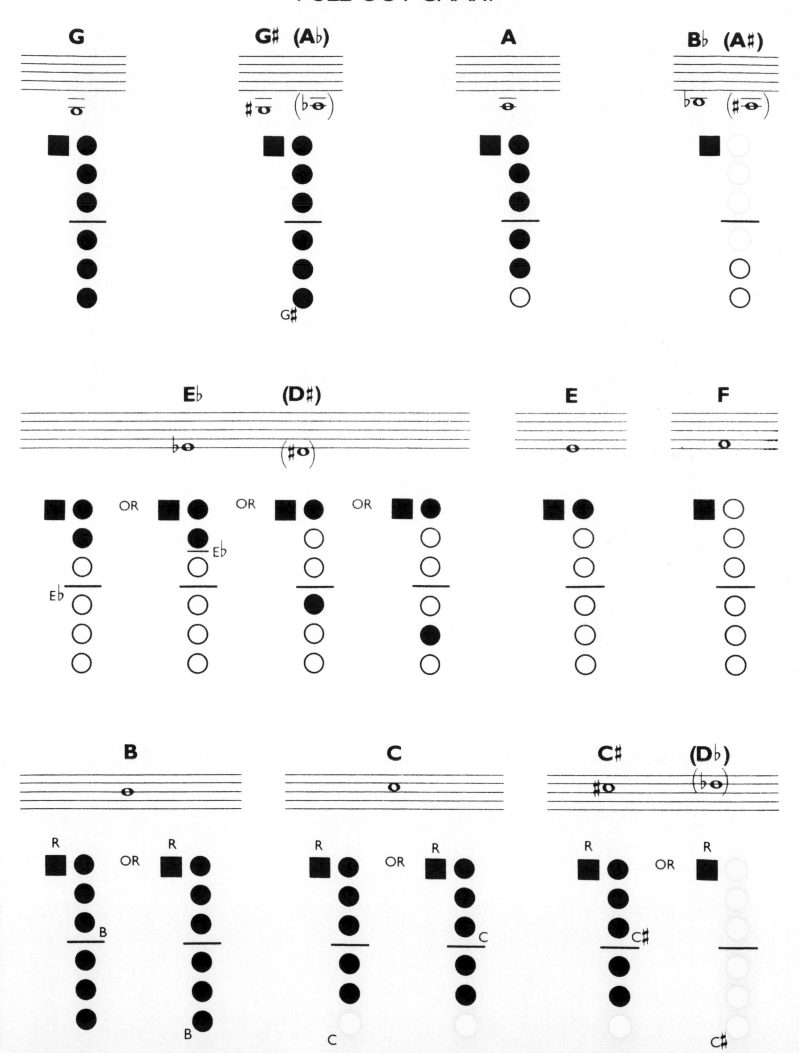

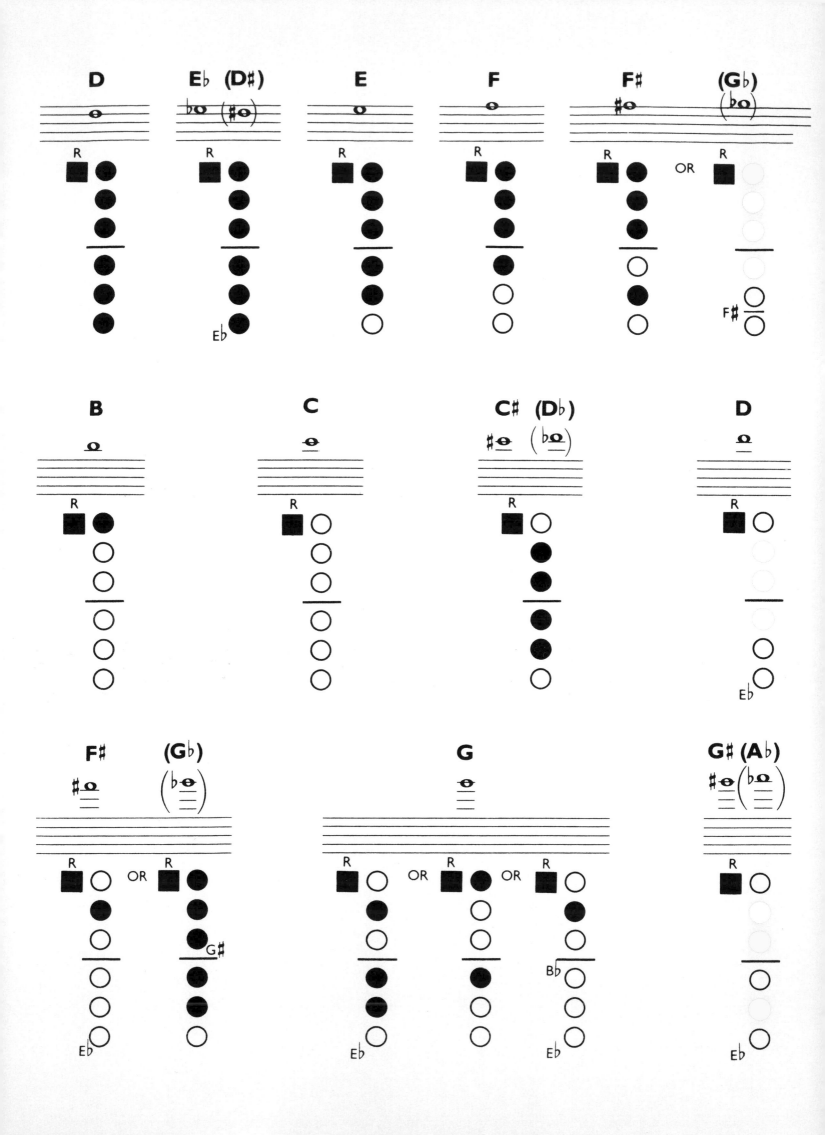

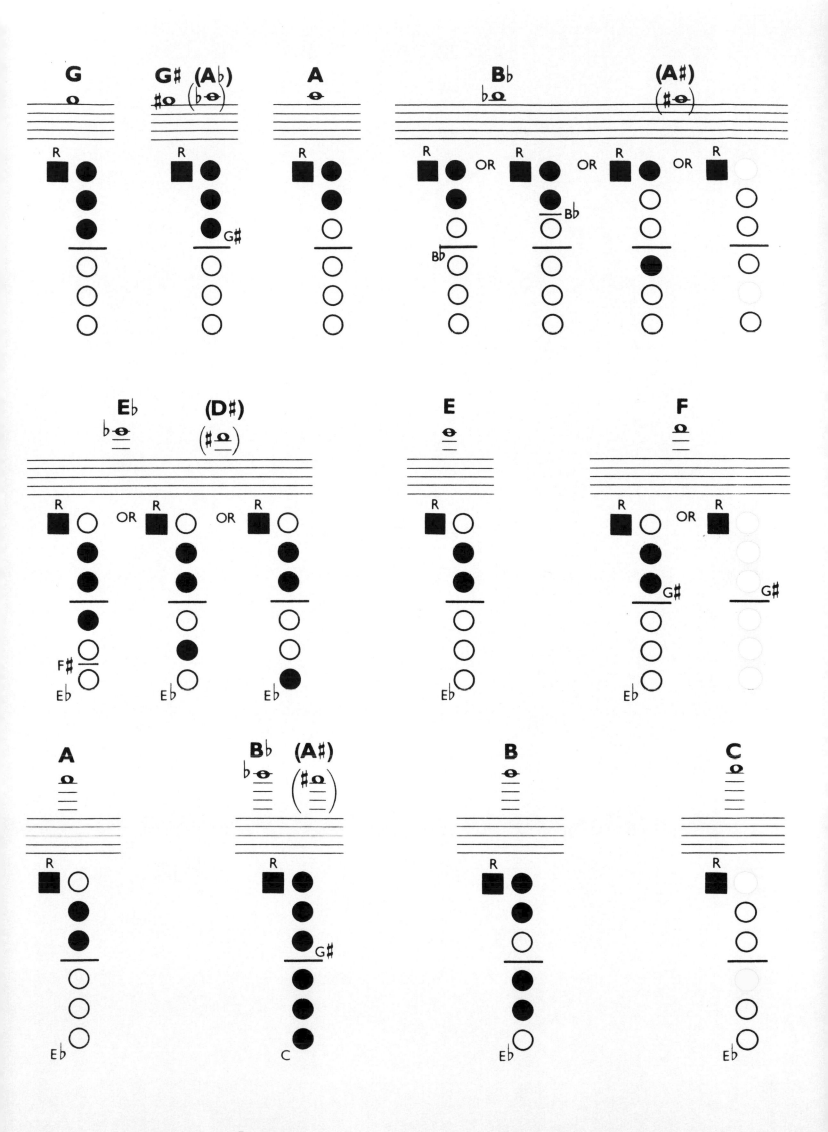

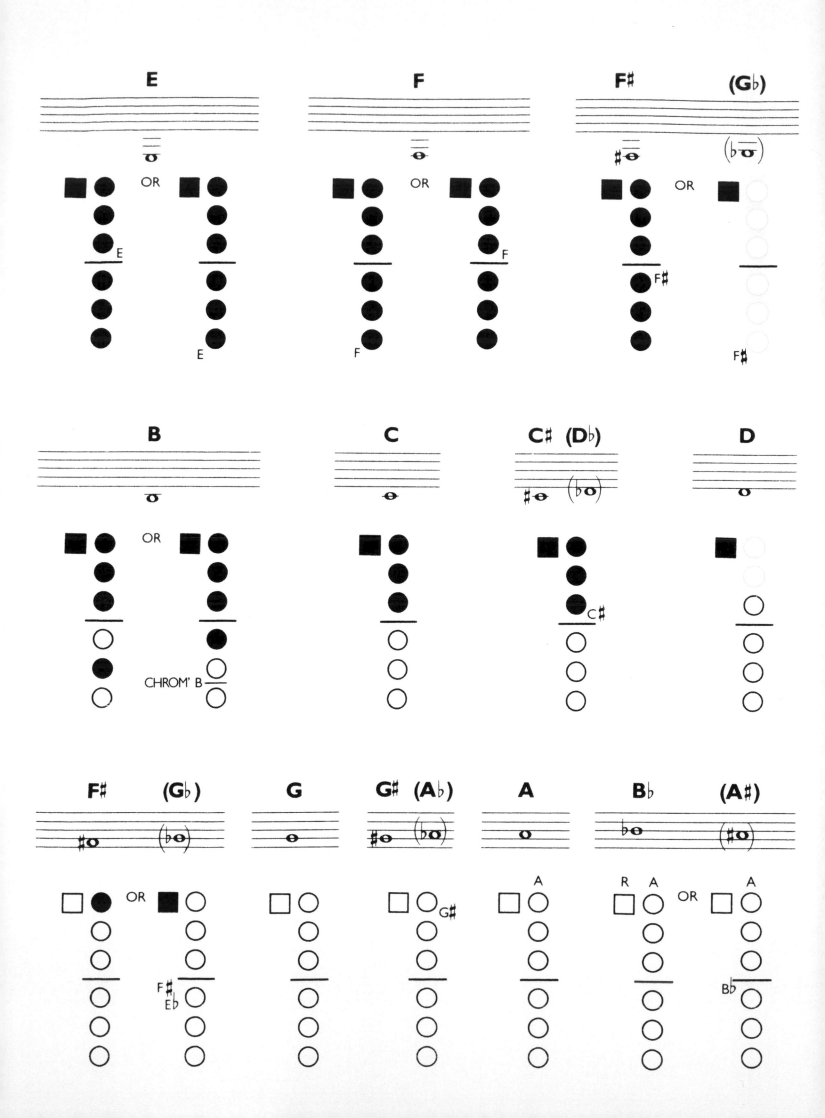

Session 6: SONGS GOING DOWN TO LOW G

To play low G, add finger no. 3.

This is an octave below open G.

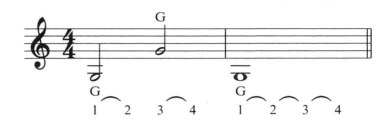

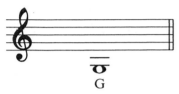

AMAZING GRACE
Traditional

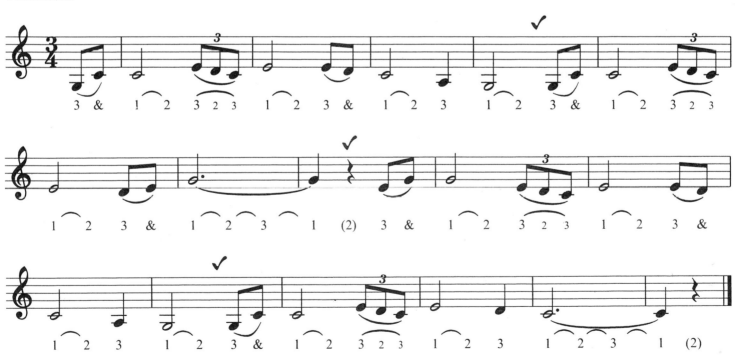

THE BALLAD OF DAVY CROCKETT

Words by Tom Blackburn   Music by George Bruns

SUR LE PONT D'AVIGNON

Traditional

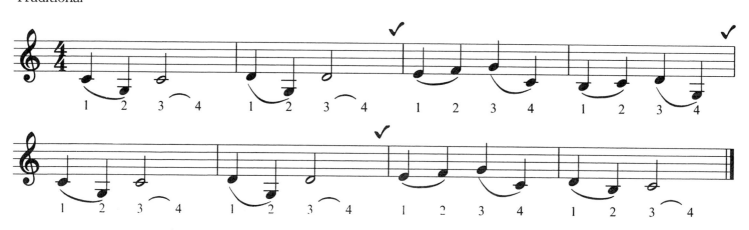

ALOUETTE
Traditional

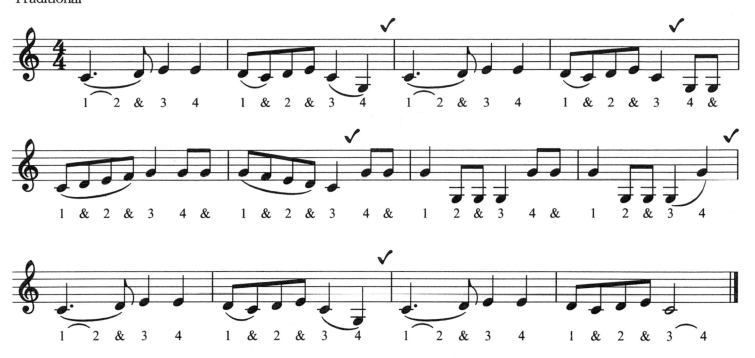

AULD LANG SYNE
Traditional

I'D LIKE TO TEACH THE WORLD TO SING

Words & Music by Roger Cook, Roger Greenaway, Billy Backer & Billy Davis

Session 7: STACCATO

Now you've learnt tonguing:

Tee Tee Tee Tee   Tee Tee Tee Tee   Tee
1 2 3 4   1 2 3 4   1 2 3 4

and slurring:

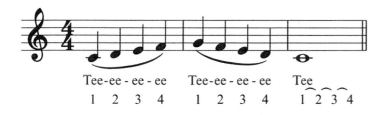

Tee-ee - ee - ee   Tee-ee - ee - ee   Tee
1   2   3   4   1   2   3   4   1 2 3 4

It's time to learn staccato, or very short notes. This is done by stopping the notes with your tongue on the reed.

Teet Teet Teet Teet   Teet Teet Teet Teet
1   2   3   4   1   2   3   4

It's important to keep blowing evenly, as if slurring, and shorten the notes with your tongue only.

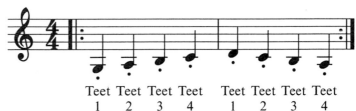

Teet Teet Teet Teet   Teet Teet Teet Teet
1   2   3   4   1   2   3   4

THE MARSEILLAISE
By Claude Joseph Rouget de Lisle

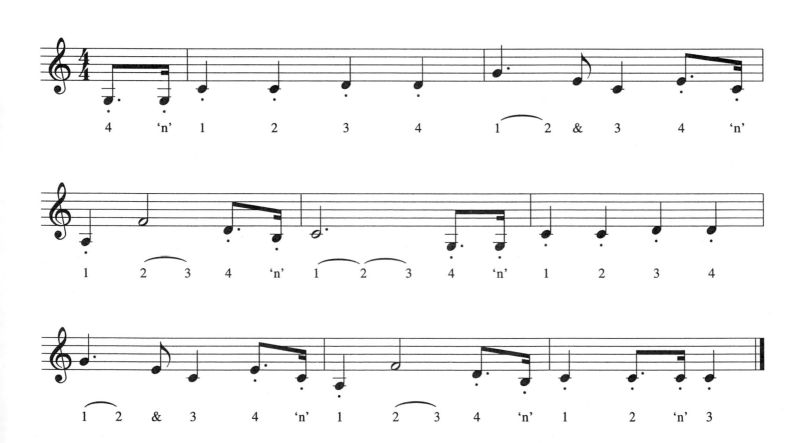

GONNA BUILD A MOUNTAIN

Words & Music by Leslie Bricusse & Anthony Newley

WHEN JOHNNY COMES MARCHING HOME

Traditional

RIVERS OF BABYLON

Words & Music by Farian, Reyam, Dowe & McMaughton

Session 8: THE KEY OF G MAJOR

A sharp sign (♯) before a note raises it a semitone or half step.

The key of G has one sharp: F♯.

This is called the key signature. Although the sharp is written on top line F only, it applies to all other F's.

The key signature, makes these F's into F♯'s as well

The first F♯ you will need is played with just the left hand finger no. 1 on the top hole (thumb off).

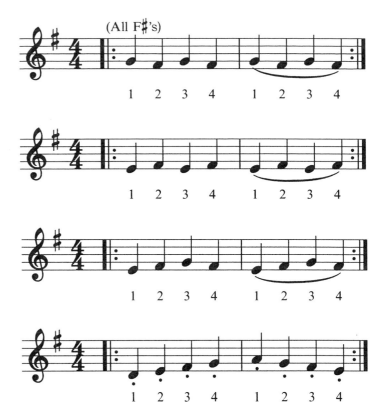

(All F♯'s)

1 2 3 4   1 2 3 4

1 2 3 4   1 2 3 4

1 2 3 4   1 2 3 4

1 2 3 4   1 2 3 4

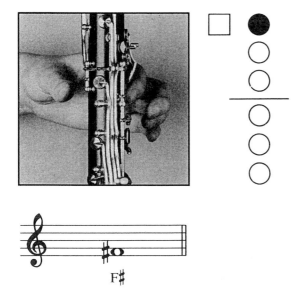

F♯

JOY TO THE WORLD
By George Frideric Handel

ON TOP OF OLD SMOKEY
Traditional

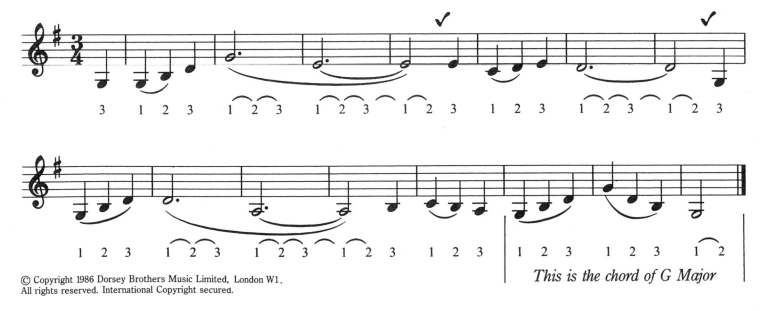

This is the chord of G Major

These two Beatle songs also illustrate the *Scale* and
Chord very well:

ALL MY LOVING
Words & Music by John Lennon & Paul McCartney

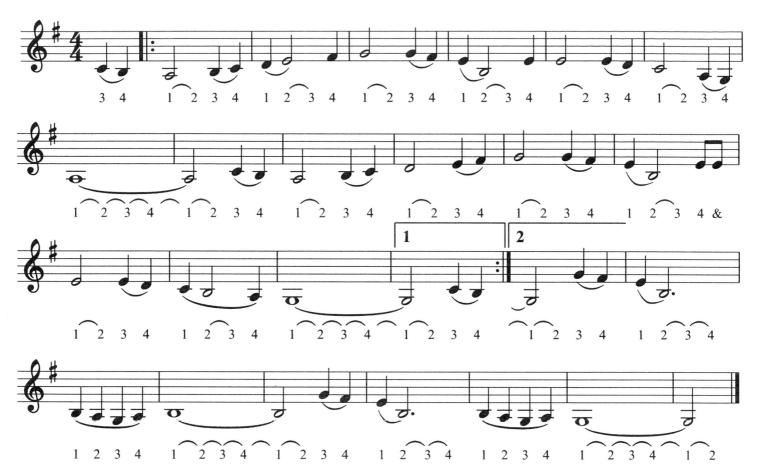

OB-LA-DI, OB-LA-DA
Words & Music by John Lennon & Paul McCartney

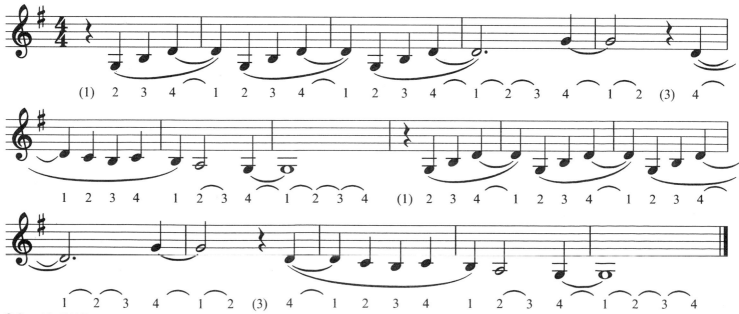

Session 9: THE KEY OF F MAJOR

Remember, a flat sign (♭) before a note lowers it a semitone or half step.

The key of F has one flat, B♭.

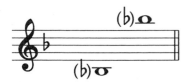

Low B♭ is played with all your left hand on, plus finger no. 1 of your right hand.

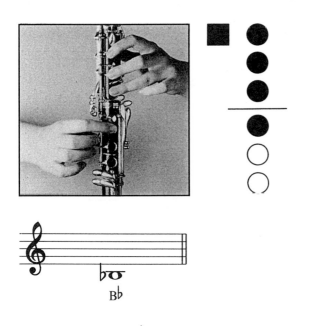

B♭

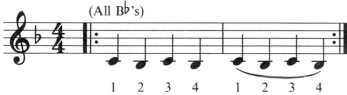

This B♭ is an octave below the B♭ you learnt in session 4.

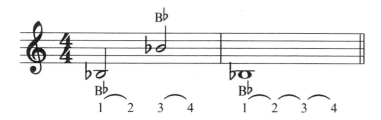

Bottom F is played with all the holes covered, plus right hand finger no. 4 (little finger) on the F key.

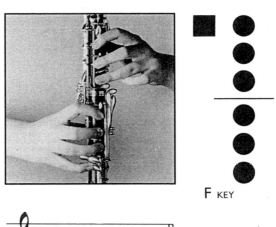

F KEY

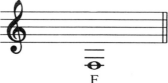

F

This F is an octave below the F you learnt in session 2.

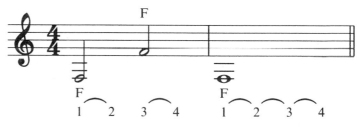

Here are some of the songs you played in Session 3 with just your left hand, for your right hand to try. But don't forget that for all notes below D you have to keep your left hand firmly closing all the holes in the top joint.

AU CLAIR DE LA LUNE
Traditional

WHEN THE SAINTS GO MARCHING IN
Traditional

THIS OLE HOUSE
Words & Music by Stuart Hamblen

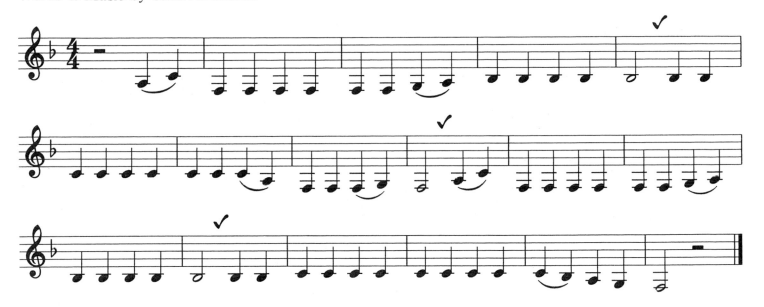

MICHAEL ROW THE BOAT ASHORE
Traditional

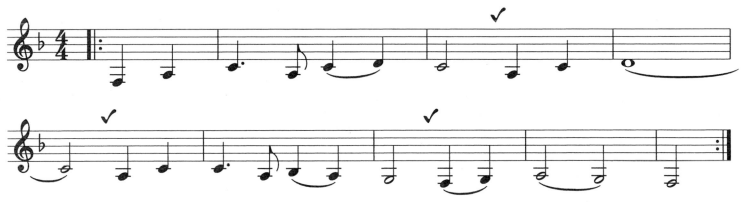

YELLOW SUBMARINE
Words & Music by John Lennon & Paul McCartney

Session 10: CLOSING THE WHOLE TUBE

The lowest note of the clarinet is bottom E: all fingers on, with left little finger (no. 4) on the E key.

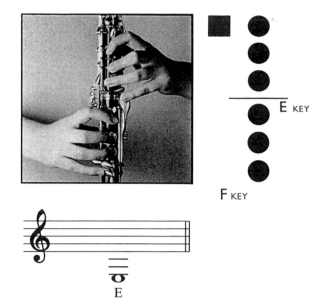

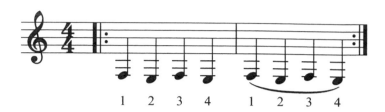

Keep your right little finger on the F key all the time.

This E is an octave below the E you learnt in Session 3.

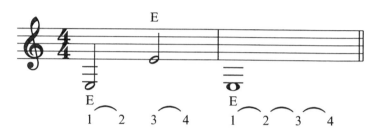

GOD SAVE THE QUEEN
Traditional

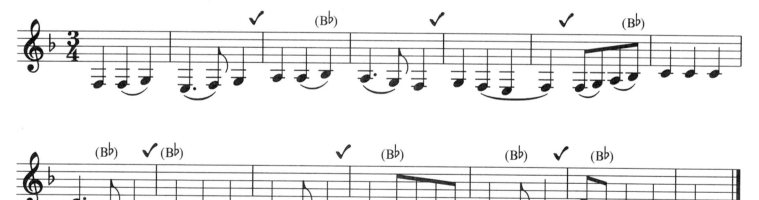

Our *Scale* and *Chord* songs in the key of F major:

JOY TO THE WORLD
By George Frideric Handel

ON TOP OF OLD SMOKEY
Traditional

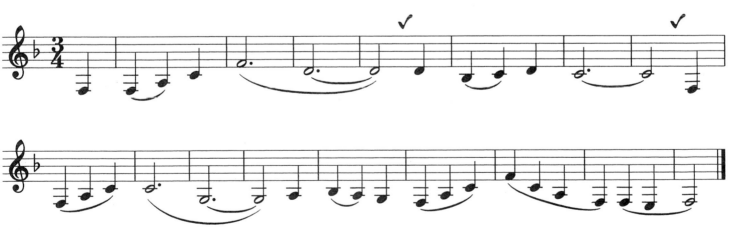

OB-LA-DI, OB-LA-DI
Words & Music by John Lennon & Paul McCartney

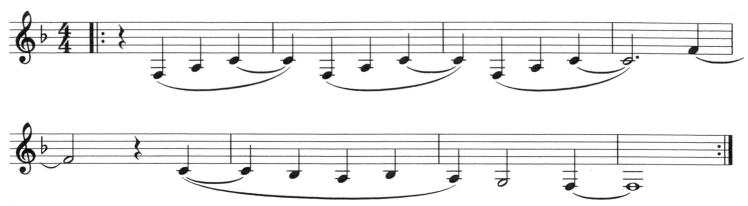

WHERE HAVE ALL THE FLOWERS GONE
Words & Music by Pete Seeger

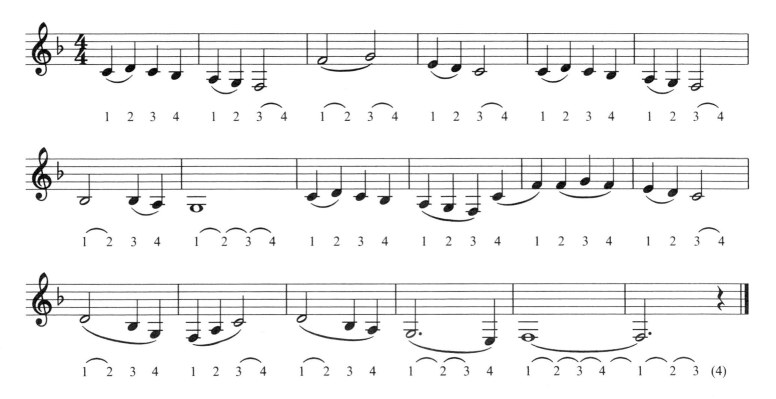

Session 11: MORE SONGS IN THE KEY OF G MAJOR

For these songs you will need low F sharp, which is fingered as for low G, plus your left little finger (no. 4) on the F sharp key.

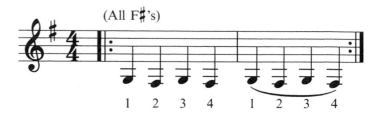
(All F♯'s)

1 2 3 4   1 2 3 4

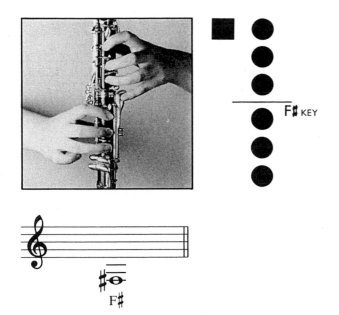

F♯ KEY

This F sharp is an octave below the F sharp you learnt in Session 8.

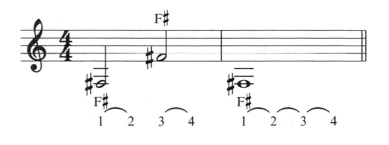
F♯
F♯   F♯
1 2 3 4   1 2 3 4

F♯

GOD SAVE THE QUEEN
Traditional

(F♯)   (F♯)

HE'S GOT THE WHOLE WORLD IN HIS HANDS

Traditional

IF I HAD A HAMMER

Words & Music by Lee Hays & Pete Seeger

DECK THE HALLS

Traditional

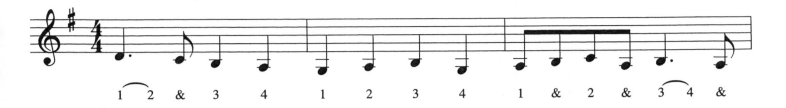

Session 12:
SONGS COVERING ALL THE BOTTOM REGISTER

You've now covered the whole range of the bottom
register. These notes enable you to play lots of songs,
especially in the key of F:

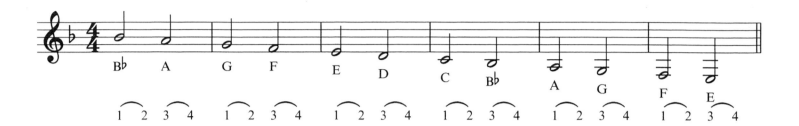

and in the key of G:

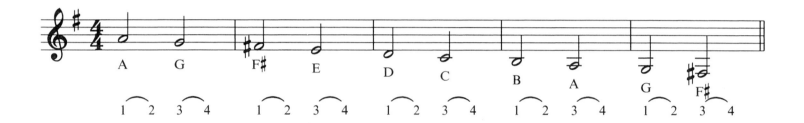

THE TWELFTH OF NEVER
Words by Paul Francis Webster   Music by Jerry Livingston

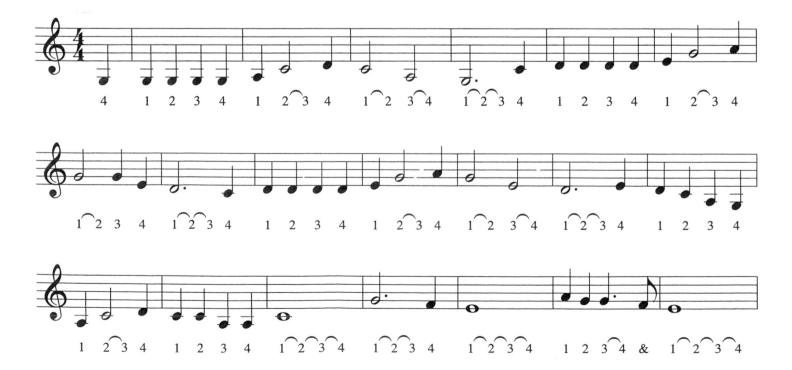

CIELITO LINDO

Traditional

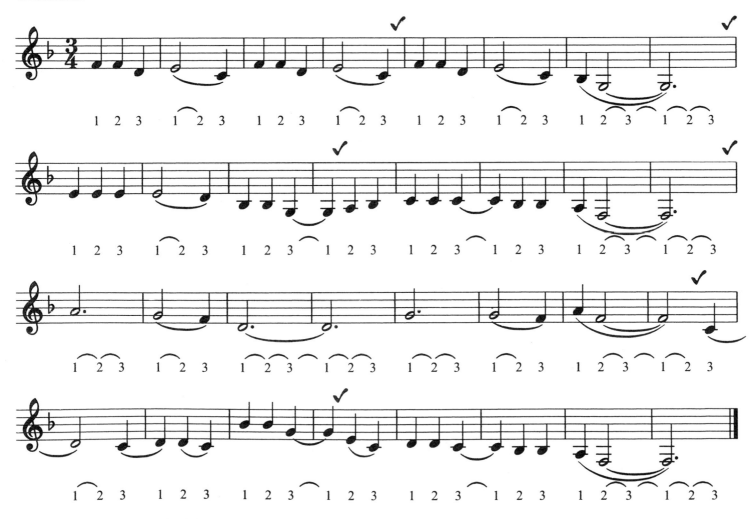

I WILL GIVE MY LOVE AN APPLE

Traditional

3 & 1 2 3 & 1 2 3   1 & 2 3   1 2   3 & 1 2 3 &

1 2 3   1 2 3   1 2 3 & 1 2 3 & 1 & 2 3

1 & 2 3   1 2 3   1 2 3   1 2 3   1 2 3   1 2

CRADLE SONG

Composed by Johannes Brahms

WITH A LITTLE HELP FROM MY FRIENDS

Words & Music by John Lennon & Paul McCartney

Congratulations on completing Book One of this course. By now you should be well on the way to becoming an accomplished clarinet player.

In Book Two you will learn the rest of the bottom register notes, play tunes using all the bottom register, start the upper register and play many popular songs including Fiddler On The Roof, Lucille and I Can't Give You Anything But Love all specially arranged to gradually extend your knowledge of the upper register comparing fingering with the bottom register.